Sharing Boundaries

Sharing Boundaries

Learning the Wisdom of Africa

Annetta Miller

SHARING BOUNDARIES: Learning the Wisdom of Africa
© Copyright 2003 by Annetta Miller
Design by Joyce Maxwell
Published by Paulines Publications Africa, Nairobi
ISBN 9966-21-899-8
Year of Publication 2003

Printed by Kolbe Press, Limuru (Kenya)

CONTENTS

The spirit of man is without boundaries.

African proverb

INTRODUCTION

Africa

Thank you

  for sharing
  your wisdom

    Through your proverbs
    through interaction with numerous
    African friends
      my boundaries
      have been stretched
           expanded
           enriched

In sharing
these vignettes
may other boundaries
be expanded
  enriched

Africa

Thank you

The proverb lover knows no boundary.

Zimbabwean proverb

PROVERBS

I called a Kenyan colleague
into my office
at Kenyatta University

    I needed advice

After explaining the situation
I waited for her response

    She waited for some time
    then responded by means
    of a proverb

Proverbs
are used throughout Africa
as a way of saying something
without spoon feeding

Proverbs
are a way of encoding the philosophical
    religious
    worldview
which mirrors the community

    "Is that all?"
    I pleaded

She nodded, rose
and walked out the door

One who greets another profits by it; one who does not, loses by it.

Ethiopian proverb

matatu   public transport van

SHAKING HANDS

The *matatu* was late
arriving at Kenyatta University

    I was in a hurry
    late for my class

Three of my colleagues
were chatting
near the classroom

I did not stop
to greet them

The next day
my colleagues chided me
for not stopping
to shake hands

    One shakes hands often
    in Africa

To shake each other's hands
is to wish
each other well

My Western haste
          efficiency
          time value
          promptness
causes me to forget
the importance
of human relationships

Too much
in a hurry
    to shake
    my colleagues' hands
    and wish them well

Good greeting is better than a good bed.

Ethiopian proverb

GREETINGS

In my Western
business-like manner
I dialed the Deputy Vice-Chancellor
of Kenyatta University
inquiring about possible housing
for a visiting lecturer
joining the music department

    After I had hastily addressed
    the issue
    I waited
    for his response

A slight
almost embarrassing pause

    then

"Good morning
How are you?
How is the family?
I haven't seen you
for a long time
How can I help you?"

A real person goes beyond himself or herself.

Tanzanian proverb

BEING

We often sat in silence
she and I

Her Swahili was limited
My Kikuyu nonexistent

It was the kindness in her eyes
the gentleness of her spirit
the generosity of her heart
the depth of her spirituality
that attracted me to her

    She could not read
    She could not write
    She spoke no English

Yet communication
was evident
    soul to soul
    spirit to spirit

The look
The bearing

The tone of her voice
    spoke of another kind
    of communication

A communication
too easily forgotten
too easily lost
by my Western busyness
        haste
        efficiency
        inability to be silent
          and listen

We often sat in silence
she and I

soul to soul
spirit to spirit

    A communication
    so easily
    found in Africa

Not all time is like the herding time.

Kenyan proverb

irio	Kikuyu dish made from mashed potatoes and greens mixed with fresh corn

TIME

Mama Maina runs
a little kiosk
in Jogoo Road market
in the Eastlands section
of Nairobi

For eight years
we were fortunate
to live next door
to this market

Mama Maina became a close friend

Nearly every day
during those eight years
I sat in her kiosk
and drank tea
and chatted in Swahili

I would at times
help her cut the meat
and peel the potatoes

for the *irio* she served

One foot was always busy
keeping the chickens at bay

The people who came
to eat her *irio*
or drink her sweet tea
became my friends

Drinking tea
in Mama Maina's kiosk
had a timelessness about it

In fact
time stopped
in the kiosk

It not only stopped
It glowed

I am because we are; we are because I am.

Swahili proverb

---

yule mzungu	that white person
matatu	public transport van

RELATIONSHIPS

*M*atatu No. 145
goes directly
to Kenyatta University

After riding the *matatu*
for many years
a kind of *matatu* community
emerged for me

There were smiles at first
then nods
then greetings
and soon the 1 ½ hours
were spent chatting with new friends
whose faces had become familiar
over the years

The *matatu* is always full
of students
with bags of books
of mamas
with sacks of cabbages and
potatoes

of soldiers
with guns
and many times
an odd chicken
cackling underfoot

I am the only white on the *matatu*
And I don't mind being called
"Yule mzungu"

I could take a taxi
or some other means of transport
It would save time

But in Africa
time is not necessarily money

Time is about
relationships

Matatu No. 145 has transported
many people
into my life

Time destroys all things.

Nigerian proverb

MAKING TIME

I walked into his office
hastily seeking information

  "Sit down,"
    he said
  "You are going to die
  of a heart attack
  like all the other white people"

I was in a hurry
a big hurry
  I thought

  But I sat down
  for several minutes
  and absorbed
  his relaxed atmosphere

He was chatting
with several refugees

  They all chided me

"Time
is something
we have plenty of here
  In Africa
  you never push time"

  But after several minutes
  I stood up to go
  and rushed on
    my busy way

Sounds are the breathing airs of the heart.
Kenyan proverb

LISTENING

The secretary
of the Dean, Faculty of Arts
at Kenyatta University
calls me on the phone
nearly every day

"Good morning,
Music Department,"
I respond

Ten seconds
into the call
she asks

"Are you there?"

I realize the importance
of participatory listening
in African conversations

To listen means
to make meaningless noises
to show participation
agreement
in the conversation

So I "hmm, hmm"
and "eeh, eeh"

She knows
I am there

23

It is a blessing to have many visitors.

Swahili proverb

HOSPITALITY

"Your coming
has been a real blessing"
   he says as we get up to leave

   My African host puts me to shame

I am reprimanded
for seeing unexpected guests
as intruders
infringing on my schedule
        my space
        my haste

  "It is always a joy
to have guests"
   he adds

The genuine warmth
of his smile
and his handshake
remind me
that hospitality
showered so liberally
in Africa
    is one of the greatest gifts
    we can offer each other

A crazy guest eats and leaves right away.

African proverb

GUEST

We had piled
too many commitments
into one day

So when we had lunch
with a Kenyan friend
we needed to excuse ourselves
soon after eating

"But why are you
leaving so soon?
We haven't even talked!"
our host reprimanded us

Eating together in Africa
is an important social function

Plenty of time is spent on drinks
                          talking
                          food

A meal is never rushed

"But can't you stay
another hour or so?"

And he shook his head
disappointedly at these Westerners
who rushed through their meal
and got up and left

even before
we had talked!

You should prepare food for a person even though the person pretends not to be hungry.

Kenyan proverb

chapati   round flat unleavened bread

FOOD

I had stopped in
to see a Kenyan friend

   I had just eaten lunch
   I was not hungry

      "Please don't cook
      I've just eaten,"
        I pleaded

But I heard her
telling the maid something
in the kitchen

   Just as I was about to leave
   the maid entered with meat
          chapatis
          rice
          greens

In Africa
food is always prepared
for a visitor

   I was overwhelmed
   and really not hungry

      "But you must eat
      I have not seen you
      for such a long time!"

Relationship is in eating together.

Ugandan proverb

---

ugali   staple food of stiff maize meal
porridge

EATING

"There is always
enough food," he said
as we were preparing to leave

    We had stopped in for a brief visit
    after the Sunday service

So we stayed
for *ugali* and cabbage stew

    The simple diet
    in many Africa homes
    provides ample food
    for numerous unexpected visitors

Several other people stopped by
and stayed for lunch

    unexpected
    yet welcome

"You see," he said
"there is always plenty of food"

*O*nly insane people eat in the street.

African proverb

matatu	public transport van
samosa	triangular, savory filled pastry

SHARING

I was returning home
from Kenyatta University

It was 4 p.m.
when I alighted
from the *matatu*
in downtown Nairobi

I was hungry
I had not eaten all day

I bought a *samosa*
to tide me over

I began eating the *samosa*
as I walked down the street
to catch *matatu* No. 23

Suddenly
a street boy
was by my side

"Give me that *samosa*,"
he pleaded

I was too hungry
to be in a sharing mood

After all
the *samosa* was small

But down deep I knew
how impolite I was
eating in public

In Africa
food is always shared

The *samosa*
did not sit well
in my stomach

That night
I was violently ill

33

He who eats with both hands will come to a bad end.

Swahili proverb

---

ugali staple food of stiff maize meal
porridge

MANNERS

A friend
from the United States
was visiting us

We were invited to dine
with Kenyan friends

ugali
beef stew
greens

all eaten
with the fingers

Our friend
new to Africa
used her right hand
then her left hand
to get a hunk of *ugali*
from the common dish

In many African societies
eating with the fingers is normal
but eating with the left hand
is forbidden

The left hand
is considered unclean

Our Kenyan friends
eyed our American friend carefully

"That one!"
    I overheard our hostess exclaim
    as I carried the dirty dishes
    to the kitchen
"That one
has no manners!"

When there is a feast everyone is welcome.

African proverb

FEASTING

We threw a feast
for numerous friends
as a way of saying farewell

In a week's time
we would leave Kenya
to live in Canada for two years

The first Kenyan friend to arrive
brought four uninvited friends

My heart sank

What if all the guests
brought uninvited friends?

Would there be enough food?

I had catered
for only a limited number

But I welcomed them
knowing that in Africa
when there is a feast
all are welcome

The excess food
embarrassingly
flooded my refrigerator
my kitchen
the following days

37

*O*ne favours him from whom one has in the past received a gift.

Kenyan proverb

GIFTS

I was visiting
a Kenyan artist friend

One of his paintings
struck my eye

"How beautiful!
How lovely!"
    I exclaimed

He removed the painting
from the wall
and gave it to me

"Oh, no, please keep it,"
    I demanded

But he insisted

In Africa
excessive complimenting

is seen as asking
for the item

The painting
    hung on my wall
    for a number of years

Many years later
someone exclaimed
about the beautiful painting
on our wall

    I took it down
    and gave it to her

In Africa
the gift always moves

You only have what you give away.

African proverb

GOODWILL

In 1987
when we left
for Canada for two years
our Kenyan friends
flocked to the airport
to wave us off

  A dear friend
  brought a basket
  filled with bananas
  and a live chicken

Africans express goodwill
through the giving
of gifts

  A farewell
  is a special occasion
  for expressing such goodwill

I thanked her kindly
and hugged goodbye

  As we were about to proceed
  to the departure lounge
  I untied the legs
  of the chicken

Somewhere
around Jomo Kenyatta International
Airport
there is a chicken . . .

Life is when you are with others, alone you are like an
animal.

Malawian proverb

ALONE

"You are all alone in this big house?"

My Kenyan friend
is astonished

"How can you stay alone?"

Harold is often away on trips
I have learned to be alone
    and even enjoy my aloneness

Our three-bedroom house
must seem enormous to her

She shares one small room
    with a friend and her husband

Two beds adorn the room
    each with a sheet
    dangling in front

Her one room is attached
    to many such rooms
    teeming with people

children
more children
chickens

My Western need for space
alienates me from people

I need at times
to be alone

Alone?

She will never be alone
She does not want it
            need it
            cherish it

She clicks her tongue
and shakes her head –

a sign of disbelief
        pity
        amazement

43

*T*here is always room for the people you love even if the house is crowded.

Tanzanian proverb

SPACE

A friend
from the United States
was visiting us recently

"Oh, what a small place
you live in!"
   he commented
   about our one-bedroom apartment

      And I remember
      his enormous house
      where he and his wife live
      alone

This evening
a Kenyan friend
stopped in for a visit

"My, what a large house!"
   he exclaimed

      And I remember
      his tiny house
      where he and his wife
      and five children
      plus members
      of the extended family
      live together

I belong by blood relationship; therefore I am.
                                    Ghanaian proverb

EXTENDED FAMILY

He came into my office one morning
informing me that his sister's husband
had been killed in the clashes

    I offered condolences

It was his responsibility
to educate and care
for his sister's son

Several days later
I inquired about his sister

    "Oh, my cousin is fine"

"But I thought
it was your sister's husband
who was killed"

His complex explanation
of his relationship to this woman
made it clear
that in Africa
little distinction is made
    between cousins and sisters
    between mothers and aunts
    between fathers and uncles

All belong
to one large
extended family

"It is by God's action that he or she died."

Swahili proverb

Mungu yuko tu	God is
Eeh, ni kweli	It's true

ACCEPTANCE

I found a note
in my mailbox
at Kenyatta University
one Tuesday morning

   "Dear Mrs. Miller
   I was not in class on Friday
   because my child died
     I hope you will excuse me"

I was surprised
when this person
turned up for the 10 a.m. class

   After class
   I sought him out
   and offered condolences

There seemed to be
a slight shrug
in his shoulders
when he replied
   "Mungu yuko tu"

It was a simple acceptance
that the cycles
of good and bad
are controlled
by a higher power

   My *"Eeh, ni kweli"*
   sounded thin
   as we walked out the door

*P*raise and truth are revealed slowly.

Ethiopian proverb

TRUTH

"It's quite far
It will take you
an hour and a half
to drive there"

We had stopped
to ask directions to a park

"But we don't have time
to travel that far,"
we told him

"Oh, well
perhaps it's only
a half hour"

Truth?
Which is the truth?

His instructions
had little to do
with reality

He had simply told us
what he thought
we wanted to hear

A hasty person misses the sweet things.

Swahili proverb

Haraka haraka haina baraka

Hurry, hurry has no blessing

HASTE

I was running
up the stairs
of Jogoo House

   I hadn't noticed him
   I hadn't been noticing anybody

I was a whole hour late
for my meeting
on the Music Festival

   I was in a hurry

"What is your rush, Mrs. Miller?"
a former student called
as I rushed past him

   Haste is the greatest sign
   of disrespect
   in much of Africa

I backed up
to exchange
a breathless greeting
but rushed on
with my Western speed

   "Haraka haraka haina baraka"
   he threw at me
   as I continued to the sixth floor

I was the first
to arrive at that meeting

   Fifteen minutes later
   the second person arrived

   An hour and a half late
   we began the meeting

Haraka haraka
haina baraka

You are a fool not to ask.

Kenyan proverb

Hodi	May I come in?
Karibu	Come in!

ASKING

"Hodi, hodi" she called
"Karibu" I replied

She came in
and sat down

How were the children?
How was my husband?
How was my work?
Why hasn't God brought the rain?

I made tea

To have a guest sit in your house
and not drink something
is unthinkable

We drank
and chatted

She was the second wife --
running a food kiosk
in Nairobi

The first wife
was on a farm
far from Nairobi
caring for the children

Because of the drought
there was no food at home
The children were suffering
Business was slack
They had no money
It was January
and there was no money for school
fees

Could I help them?

The little bit I gave
could hardly meet
her needs

But the smile on her face
was a smile
of hope

The salesperson does not have only one door.

Tanzanian proverb

BARGAINING

"Five hundred shillings"
    he said
      as I picked out a basket

"Two hundred,"
    I countered

"Four hundred"

   "Two hundred"

"Three hundred and fifty"

   "Two hundred"

In Africa
bargaining is never
just selling and buying

It constitutes
a relationship
between two people

The outcome
must be pleasing to both
to ensure
that the relationship continues

"OK, two hundred and fifty"

   "OK, two hundred and fifty"

   He laughed
   slapped my hand
   in jovial affirmation
   and handed me the basket

A dog that steals is paid by a stroke of the cane.

Ugandan proverb

INSTANT JUSTICE

Two thieves
ran through
Kenyatta University campus
trying to escape outside villagers

   In no time
   the students converged
   on these thieves

One was beaten to death
The other burned to death

   It happened so quickly
   I only heard about it
   after the incident

Instant justice
is common on the streets
of Nairobi

   Is it urban boredom
   Or does it stem from respect
   for property rights

   in the village
   making stealing
   a violation
   of the village code?

I left campus that day
downhearted

   Had I been on the scene
   could I as an expatriate
   as a peace-loving Mennonite
   have done anything
   to stop the killings?

What would I have done?

   I do not know

But the least I could do now
was to grieve with the other students
who also grieved
over such brutal
loss of life

To give to your friend is not to cast away, it is to store for the future.

Swahili proverb

GENEROSITY

This afternoon
my husband and I
bought fifteen trees to plant
at a Kenyan friend's farm

Our friend
gave eight of the trees
to his neighbour

Sharing
giving
generosity
are all a part
of African culture

After we had finished
planting the trees
our friend
leaned on a fencepost

"So, my friend,"
he said to the young neighbour
"you'll now make sure
that I have enough firewood
in my old age!"

Peace is good soil for man to grow.

African proverb

PEACE

Every year
my husband and I
plant several trees
on a Kikuyu friend's farm
outside Nairobi

    The first trees
    we planted are now
    over thirty feet tall

This year
I looked over into the farm
adjoining our friend's
land

    A neat row of young trees
    was spreading its branches

"Yes," he said,
"your tree planting
is contagious

But I gave my neighbor
the first trees to plant

If I hadn't done that
he would be very jealous of my trees

    This way
    there is
    no jealousy
    and there is
      peace"

One must always have the habit of sharing and going to those who are afflicted.

Congolese proverb

COMPASSION

For a week
Harold lay in Nairobi Hospital
deliriously ill with high fever

It was a mutant chloroquine-resistant
strain of malaria
which he had picked up
in Zambia

For three of those days
he hovered
between life and death

Those days
although filled
with strain and worry
were days
filled with
the warmest human encounters
we have ever experienced

Our African friends
came to the hospital
and just sat with us

How well they know
the meaning
of supportive compassion

And during the five weeks
of Harold's recovery
our house was filled
with their warmth

Theirs is the gift
of compassionate sharing

A sharing that
gives of one's self
A giving that
weeps with those who weep
and suffers with those who suffer

A gift bestowed on us
in abundance

Reconciliation is deeper in eating together.

Sudanese proverb

---

ugali   staple food of stiff maize meal
               porridge

RECONCILIATION

Something happened
in the Music Department
which deeply upset me

   In my frustration
   I wrote a letter
   to the Dean
   expressing that annoyance

The Kenyan chairman
of the Music Department
calmly invited me to lunch
in the Common Room
of Kenyatta University

He never mentioned
the conflict

But somehow
in that simple meal
of *ugali* and cabbage stew

   peace was restored

When spider webs unite, they can tie up a lion.

Ethiopian proverb

COOPERATION

Yesterday
I was invited to lunch
at the Canadian High Commissioner's
residence

　　Seven of us
　　sat around the table

My Kenyan friend
had invited me to the luncheon

　　"We are having trouble
　　with one of the ladies
　　who is trying
　　to make financial gain
　　through our association,"
　　　she told me

In Africa
one never tackles
a problem alone

It is always
a group effort

Throughout the meal
those present made remarks
about donating time
　　　　　money
　　　　　talent
　　　　　　　towards the efforts
　　　　　　　of the association

After the meal
the culprit
apologized
and offered her services
free

　　During the ride home
　　my friend slapped my hand
　　and laughed heartily

　　　"You see –
　　　it worked!"

69

Happiness is openness to all people.

African proverb

WISDOM

"How do you do it?"
I enquired
of a long–standing Kenyan friend

    A wise man
    A loved man
    An extremely busy man

I was feeling bogged down
stressed, annoyed
with endless administration
with corruption
with the streams of people
filling my office
at Kenyatta University
seeking monetary assistance

    His words
    were words of wisdom

"I never turn anyone away
I listen to all
I give to all who ask"

In Africa
wisdom is being aware
of others

A wise person
helps others

    I shook my head
    In amazement

    He has streams and streams
    of people flooding his office daily

He is wise
He is happy

    He is open to all people

My house is like a spongy coconut; anyone who likes goes into it.

African proverb

SUCCESS

Our Kenyan friend,
is a source of amazement
and inspiration

   He knows everyone
   He is generous
   He helps everyone
   He is successful

In Africa
a successful person
is not necessarily measured
in terms of economic wealth

Success is centered
on the life of the community

Material goods
are to be shared with others

Selfishness
belongs to the witches
               sorcerers
               anti-people

   "Please come on Sunday
   and have lunch with us,"
   he invited

Sunday

   Twenty-odd people
   flooded his small house
   and laughed and talked
   and ate heartily

He is a loved man
known by all

   That Sunday -
   like every other Sunday -
   his house was filled
   to overflowing

We dance, therefore we are.

African proverb

RHYTHM

Every Saturday morning
my husband and I
clean the house
to the music
of Bach, Vivaldi, Mozart

    The Kenyan gardener
    outside our house is subjected
    to our choice of music

One morning
I played a tape
of African beat

    "Oh," he said
    "now that is music!"

Rhythm
in Africa
is what harmony is
to the West

    And his gardening
    took on the rhythm
      the dance
      the throb
        of the soul
        of Africa

Birds of different rivers chatter differently.

Ethiopian proverb

---

matatu   public transport van
Ni uchawi   It's witchcraft

MUSIC

The *matatu* was fairly crowded
as I squeezed into place.

   I was on my way
   to rehearse the Nairobi orchestra
   in preparation for a rendition
   of Brahms' Requiem

I opened the large conductor's score
and mentally rehearsed
some of the difficult spots

   The man across from me
   nudged his partner
   and asked in Swahili
   "Is that a book?"
      "Indeed, it is a book
      but what kind of a book?"

Then the lady sitting next to me
peered over my shoulder for a long
time
and then whispered to her neighbour
"Ni uchawi"

Although I understood the
conversations around me
I chose to remain silent
   How could I explain the complicated
   notation
   of a conductor's score
   in the twenty minute's ride?

How could I explain
that the piece of music --
a great spiritual impact
on my life --
was by no means witchcraft?

      ...

...

How could I explain
that in the West we separate
   the composer,
   the performer,
   the conductor?

How could I explain
that I was taking the role
of the conductor
to prepare the performers
to sing and play
for a totally silent audience?

How could I explain
that this large book
was full of symbols
written as a map, a blueprint?

How could I explain
that the singers
could not sing without it
the instrumentalists
could not play without it?
and that I could not even rehearse
or conduct without it?

Is it witchcraft?

If birds travel without coordination, they beat each others' wings.

Swahili proverb

COMMUNITY

We were at the coast
attending a meeting

One afternoon I wandered
through the coconut palms
toward the drums
in the distance

The village
was in a celebrative mood

drumming
dancing
ululating

In Africa
it is no small thing
to dance in community

Dancing together
is therapeutic

Dancing together
is a way of restoring harmony

No leader
all danced in a circle

tightly knit

sweating
stomping
moving

I remained
at a distance
not wanting to be
an intruding audience
in this display
of communal spirit

*W*hen there is dancing, it is not only the living who are present.

African proverb

DANCE

A dance troupe
from Kenya's coastal province
held a workshop
for the Music Department
of Kenyatta University

One of the older dancers
suddenly went into a trance
succumbing to forces
beyond his control

Trance
in an Africa dance
signals the presence
of spirits who are attracted
to the dance

Dancing
thus becomes a way
of communication
with the invisible world

A way of restoring harmony
and keeping in tune
with one's inner nature
and the cosmos

The trembling man
reconnected with the material world
and danced towards me

"*Njoo, karibu* -- join us!"
he pleaded

"I don't know how
to move my shoulders!"
I protested

Songs learned from outside sources are not used at a dance so long.

Swahili proverb

SOUNDS

I was visiting
my birthplace
near Musoma, Tanzania

   A few women
   who had been taught
   by my mother
   stopped by to chat
   one afternoon

I accompanied them
to a nearby village
to meet with a friend
who had recently given birth
   As we trudged
   the narrow path
   one woman commented

"Your mother -
she would sing
like this!"

   And she demonstrated
   with a high vibrato-laden voice

Vibrato
a sign of relaxation
of the vocal cords

An indoor sound

   As we neared the village
   she ululated three times
   a shrill, piercing sound
   of joy and jubilation

             ...

...

An outdoor sound
so common
in Africa

And I imitated her
trying desperately to erase
that indoor vibrato
from my western voice

She turned
shook her head
and laughed

A woman should never whistle.

Ugandan proverb

WHISTLING

I was whistling a tune
from Mozart's Requiem
one morning as I cleaned my desk
at Kenyatta University

   I often whistle
   while I work

The elderly male Kenyan cleaner
looked at me in shock
and reprimanded me
by shaking his head and finger

   Was I cleaning my desk
   the wrong way?

   I kept on whistling

In Africa
whistling is forbidden
for females

Then he pointed
to his lips
and pointed to mine
and shook his finger again

   I stopped whistling

The tune
inside my head
squelched
to solitary
inner hearing

One who has given birth does not wither.

Cameroonian proverb

CHILDREN

My husband and I
purposely waited six years
before we had our firstborn

My African friends
shook their heads
with despair, sadness

"God will someday bless you,"
they said
"Keep praying"

In Africa
the worst thing
that can happen to a person
is to die without descendants
thus breaking the link
between the ancestors
and the living

So when I finally gave birth
my African friends were ecstatic
"God has finally
answered your prayers!"
they exclaimed

Naming a child is inviting ancestors home.

Kenyan proverb

NAMES

When our youngest son was born
we named him immediately
    A name
    we had previously chosen

        An African friend
        was shocked

            "How can you name
            your child so quickly?
            How do you know
            his character so soon?"

In Africa
names give individuals
a position in the community

        Names are often taken
        from deceased relatives
        linking the born
        with the dead

Would my African friend
be shocked to learn
that our son decided
to use his middle name
instead of his first
when he was fifteen

        I'm sure
        he would have said
            "You see
            You should have waited"

The buying of a wife begins from a little thing.

Kenyan proverb

BRIDE PRICE

"**A**re they married?"
the old man pointed his chin
at my son and his girl friend

  "Not yet" I replied

He had stopped at the gate
to collect old newspapers
                bottles
                tins

"How many cows
                goats
                sheep
must he pay
to marry her?"

"None," I replied

"None?
And she's an educated girl?"

  A bride price
  is an assumption
  before African weddings
  take place

  Educated girls
  are more expensive

His disbelief was evident

"Not even a goat?!"

A person is a person through other persons.
African proverb

ADULTHOOD

When our eldest son
neared puberty
A Kenyan friend asked

    "When will you
    have your son circumcised?"

"Oh, our culture
doesn't have such rituals,"
    I replied

In Africa
the relationship
between the individual
and the community
finds expression
through the rites of passage

The community takes on
the responsibility
to make each adolescent
fully human

    "But how will you know
    when he has become a man?"
      she asked

An old calabash is still useful.

Malian proverb

OLD AGE

"Can you really
do that to your mother,
the one who gave birth?"
my Kenyan friend chided

    I had been describing
    the modern efficiency
    of a retirement home
    where my 89-year-old mother lives

"Is there no respect
for your mother,
for old age,
in your country?"
    she asked

    "But she's happy there"
    I affirmed

(Do I really know
the mind of my mother?)

Old age
fruitful age
hard-earned age

    respected
    cherished
    loved
    included
    tended

        by all one's relatives
        in Africa

Death is an occasion for seeking more life.

African proverb

DEATH

An aunt of mine
recently died
at the age of 87

   "Ah," my Kenyan friend commented
   "she is now your ancestor"

Dying
in Africa
is not a radical break
from life

It is a continuation
of that mysterious life force

It is a linkage
with descendants
and the living community

"She will now
have more influence
on you and your community,"
she continued

The memories of my aunt
flood my thoughts
with happiness and peace

The dead are alive and working.

Sudanese proverb

uji   porridge

ANCESTORS

We were invited
to a goat roast
at a Kenyan friend's farm

    roasted goat
    mashed potatoes
    boiled cabbage
    fermented *uji*

Our friend
poured a bit
of the *uji*
on the ground
before he drank it

    "For the ancestors,"
      he said

Life in Africa
consists of the living
      the unborn

the living-dead
    those ancestral spirits
who guard
    nurture
guide
    the living
in all that is
valuable

A pathway
between this
world
and the next

"A libation
to acknowledge their presence,"
      he said

The witch is inside the house.

Tanzanian proverb

SPIRITS

A Kenyan colleague of mine
at Kenyatta University
was hospitalized for a few days

Diabetes
the doctor diagnosed

Because she and I
had been upset
with a male colleague
she explained her illness

"He used witchcraft on me"

Africans refer to spirits
to explain why things happen
the way they do

Spirits
are to African traditional thought
what material particles
are to Western scientific thought

A week later
I come down with the flu

"You see," she said
"even you are subjected
to those spirits
He's the one
who did it"

She clicked her tongue
and jutted her jaw
in the direction
of his office

*N*obody wants to meet an ill-omened bird.

Kenyan proverb

METAPHYSICAL FORCE

A bird was singing
loudly outside our living room

  As it continued
  a Kenyan friend
  who was sipping tea with us
  commented

    "What is that bird
    trying to tell us?"

And I am reminded
that in Africa
there is the belief
that all beings
animate and inanimate
have and are life forces

  To me
  the bird was just singing

To him
the bird was a carrier
of metaphysical knowledge -
a vital force
to be reckoned with

Suddenly
the bird flitted
into our living room
and into the kitchen

  Our friend was shocked

    "Indeed!
    What can this bird
    be telling us?"

You cannot do anything unless God is there.

Ghanaian proverb

Mungu yuko tu   God is

GOD

Yesterday
I greeted a Kenyan friend
while shopping at the supermarket

   "Eeh," she said
   "Mungu yuko tu"

I am constantly amazed
at how often Africans
refer to God

   In the midst of drought
     "God is"
   In the midst of poverty
     "God is"
   In the midst of war
     "God is"
   In the midst of death
     "God is"

In Africa
religion permeates all of life

The spiritual and secular
are one

   Secular
   is the spiritual taking form

"We are still eating and alive,"
    she continued
"God is"

   And she plopped
   two cartons of milk
   into her shopping basket

A *cock cannot crow in a foreign country.*

Ugandan proverb

ABOUT THE AUTHOR

Annetta Miller, an American citizen, was born and grew up in Tanzania. She has spent nearly 50 years in Tanzania, Sudan and Kenya, having lived in Nairobi since 1974.

From 1979 to 1987 and from 1989 to 1996 she taught in the Music Department of Kenyatta University and for two of those years was the Chairperson of the department. From 1987 to 1989 she taught in the Music Department of Conrad Grebel College, University of Waterloo in Waterloo, Ontario, Canada. From 1996 to 2000 she taught in the Music Department of Daystar University.

She and her husband, Harold, are affiliated with Mennonite Central Committee and are currently working as Country Representatives for Sudan.